Exploring
new tastes

To my children, Nicholas, Lara and Scarlett

Exploring new tastes

Introduce your baby to new flavours and textures

annabel karmel

1 3 5 7 9 10 8 6 4 2

Text copyright © Annabel Karmel 2001, 2003, 2005, 2010, 2011, 2013
Photographs copyright © Dave King 2005, 2010, 2011, 2013,
except page 19 Daniel Pangbourne 2001
This edition copyright © Eddison Sadd Editions 2013

The Random House Group Limited Reg. No. 954009

A CIP catalogue record for this book is available from the British Library

ISBN: 978-009-195577-9

Printed in Hong Kong

Eddison•Sadd Editions
CREATIVE DIRECTOR Nick Eddison   INDEXER Dorothy Frame
SENIOR EDITOR Katie Golsby   DESIGNER Brazzle Atkins
PROOFREADER Nikky Twyman   ILLUSTRATIONS Nadine Wikenden
PRODUCTION Sarah Rooney
COVER PHOTOGRAPHY Dave King

Notes on the text:
· For fan-assisted ovens, reduce the temperature by 20°C.
· All black pepper is freshly ground.

Contents

Introduction

Between six and nine months, once first tastes have been accepted, you can start to increase the amount and variety of food you give your baby. She is now likely to be taking regular meals each day, but it is important to let her set the pace – every baby is different when it comes to how much they want to eat. Your baby will be developing quite rapidly at this stage. At seven months, most babies still need support when sitting and have yet to cut their first tooth; however, by nine months, it's likely that your baby will be sitting unsupported and possibly have a few teeth. This means that during this phase she will develop rapidly when it comes to eating.

This book aims to guide you through introducing new textures and flavours, to ensure that the foods you offer are compatible with your baby's stage of development. This section looks at the types of foods to try, and how to go about it.

Introducing meat, chicken and fish

The second stage of weaning marks the introduction of a wide range of foods. Babies grow more rapidly in their first year than at any other time in their life; beyond six months it isn't enough to continue giving just fruit and vegetables, as they are low in calories. At this age, babies also need nutrient-dense foods. Chicken and other meats are unlikely to cause allergies and, as they are a good source of iron, they should form a significant part of your baby's diet.

To begin with, it's a good idea to mix chicken or meat with something sweet flavoured, such as a root vegetable or a fruit like dried apricot or apple. (Avoid apricots treated with sulphur dioxide, as they can trigger asthma attacks in susceptible babies.) Slow-cooking meat – in a beef casserole, for example – is a great way to ensure that the meat is tender.

Babies are born with a store of iron inherited from their mother. At six months this begins to run low, so it's important to introduce foods containing iron from an early stage. Meat, particularly red meat, is the most easily absorbed source; however, it can also be found in leafy green vegetables and pulses such as lentils. These plant sources aren't as easily absorbed by the body. Serving them with a source of vitamin C, such as broccoli or citrus fruit, can aid absorption.

Fish is another important food for babies. Some children grow up disliking fish, so I try to make it more appealing by combining it with stronger tastes such as carrots, cheese or tomatoes. Oily fish like salmon is particularly important for the development of the brain, nervous system and vision.

Eggs

Eggs are a healthy source of protein and are rich in nutrients. They should be introduced around six to seven months, once your baby is happily taking solids. Many people avoid giving egg yolk until the age of one year, but this offers no benefit and may even increase the risk of an egg allergy. The whole egg should be cooked until solid. Why not try well-cooked scrambled egg or omelette with cheese and tomato?

Cereal and pasta

Your baby can now have 'adult' cereals like porridge and Weetabix. Cook the porridge with milk according to the packet instructions, then blend in a fruit purée.

Try cooking some small pasta shapes and stirring them into your baby's purées so that he starts to learn to chew.

Nuts

Guidelines regarding nuts have changed and you can now introduce very finely ground nuts and nut butters like peanut butter from six months. Research indicates that early introduction (after six months) may even help to prevent allergies, although this hasn't yet been confirmed. If there is a family history of allergies or eczema, watch your baby carefully after she has had anything nut-based. Never give whole nuts to children under the age of five.

Dairy products

From six months, your baby's diet can include cow's milk, cheese, butter and yoghurt. Babies grow rapidly and should be given full-fat milk and dairy products. Choose pasteurized cheeses and avoid blue cheese, Brie and Camembert. It's a good idea to combine vegetable purées with a little grated cheese such as Cheddar or Parmesan.

What to do about milk

Between six months and one year, your baby should have 500–600 ml (17–21 fl oz) of breast milk or infant formula milk per day. Cow's milk isn't as rich in vitamins and iron so shouldn't be given as your baby's main drink. However, from six months, it's fine to give cow's milk with cereal and to use it in cooking. Make sure you use full-fat milk, as babies need a high-calorie, low-fibre diet to support their rapid growth.

Drinks

Your baby can now drink tap water – it doesn't need to be boiled after six months – or very diluted fruit juice (left undiluted, it is very acidic and bad for young teeth). Around nine months, you can start offering a cup rather than a bottle; this will encourage your baby to learn to sip. Some babies love the comfort of a bottle and run the risk of filling up on milk, then not eating enough solids. Giving a cup rather than a bottle will help to avoid this.

New textures and flavours

Once your baby is confidently eating purées, start to make the consistency thicker and introduce soft lumps. This needs to be done carefully, as surprise lumps in a purée can really put off a little one. Try adding baby pasta shapes to one of your baby's favourite purées.

You can also start adding more adventurous flavours. At this stage, it is important to avoid salt (*see pages 12–13*), sugar and honey, but adding ingredients such as garlic, herbs and spices will help the transition to the food that you eat. Plus, many of these foods have valuable nutritional benefits.

Babies tend to eat quite well between six and twelve months, so this age is a real window of opportunity during which to get them to try new flavours. Not only will this ensure that your baby gets all the necessary vitamins and minerals; it will also help to reduce the chances of him becoming a fussy eater when he is older.

Salt

Before the age of one year, babies shouldn't be given any salt. As well as not adding salt to food, it's important to avoid using ingredients that are high in salt, such as ordinary stock cubes. You can buy salt-free baby stock cubes in supermarkets, or you can make your own stock. When cooking foods like pasta or rice, don't add salt to the cooking water.

Recipe information

Each recipe is accompanied by helpful information on preparation and cooking times, how many portions the recipe makes and whether it's suitable for freezing. Preparation times and portion quantities should be used as a guide only, as these will vary.

On pages 92–3, you will find a meal planner to help you to stay organized. This is intended to be used for guidance; you can, of course, use different recipes if you wish.

FIRST FINGER FOODS

Getting your little one to start feeding herself is an exciting step in her discovery of different foods. Babies are often very keen to get stuck in. At six months, hand–eye coordination isn't sufficiently developed for your baby to be able to feed herself successfully enough to get all the nutrients she needs, but it's a good idea to give her a selection of soft finger foods to experiment with alongside the purées you're feeding her. The more she tries to feed herself, the quicker she'll master the art. It's not only good for developing her hand–eye coordination; it's also a great way to introduce new flavours and textures.

Progressing to finger foods isn't a pretty process. There will be food going everywhere! I would lay a clean plastic mat on the floor under your baby's high chair, to make cleaning up a bit easier. By around nine months, most babies have developed more coordination and are able to pick up food using a pincer movement and feed themselves. Allowing them to do this is a great way to help them become more dextrous.

Safe foods to choose

With finger foods, as with any foods, there is a choking hazard, so it is important to stay with your baby while she is eating. It is advisable to avoid giving small pieces of food that could easily block the throat, such as whole grapes or hard raw vegetable sticks that can break into small, hard pieces. Start with foods that are quite soft, for example:

- Soft ripe fruit, skinned, such as pear, mango, banana, avocado or melon
- Steamed vegetables, like broccoli florets or carrot
- Toast soldiers or breadsticks
- Cooked pasta shapes

Finger foods get funky

When your baby is a bit older and has more control over her movements – and more food goes in her mouth than in her hair or on the wall – you can be a bit more adventurous. Try some of the following:

- Wafer-thin cooked meats, rolled up
- Sticks of cheese
- Raw vegetable sticks such as cucumber or sugar snap peas
- Fruit such as peeled apple slices or strawberries
- Baked sweet-potato wedges
- Rice cakes, pitta bread or bagels
- Dips such as houmous (for the vegetables and bread)
- Mini meatballs or burgers
- Pieces of chicken of fish
- Mini sandwiches, filled with cream cheese, sliced turkey or mashed banana
- Mini homemade pizzas (you could use an English muffin or tortilla wrap as the base, as well as a standard pizza base)
- Mini ice lollies made from fresh fruit or yoghurt
- Pancakes
- Dried fruit such as apricots

Vegetables

Potato, leek, carrot and pea purée

Melt the butter in a saucepan and sauté the leek for 3–4 minutes. Add the potato and carrot and pour over the stock. Bring to the boil, then reduce the heat, cover and simmer for 10 minutes. Add the frozen peas and continue to cook until the vegetables are tender (about 6 minutes). Purée in a food processor.

🖊 6 MINUTES
🍳 20 MINUTES
🍽 4 PORTIONS
❄ SUITABLE FOR FREEZING

25 g (1 oz) unsalted butter
60 g (2 oz) leeks, washed and sliced
175 g (6 oz) potatoes, peeled and cut into chunks
1 medium carrot (100 g/ 3½ oz), peeled and sliced
300 ml (½ pint) unsalted chicken or vegetable stock
50 g (2 oz) frozen peas

Frozen vegetables like peas can be just as nutritious as fresh, since they are frozen within hours of being picked. This locks in vital nutrients. Once cooked, they can be refrozen.

Eat-your-greens purée

 7 MINUTES

▦ 25 MINUTES

🍴 4 PORTIONS

❄ SUITABLE FOR FREEZING

15 g (½ oz) unsalted butter
½ small onion (40 g/
  1½ oz), peeled and
  chopped
250 g (9 oz) potatoes, peeled
  and cut into chunks
375 ml (13 fl oz) unsalted
  vegetable stock or water
50 g (2 oz) broccoli florets
50 g (2 oz) frozen peas

Melt the butter in a saucepan, then sauté the onion until softened but not coloured (about 5 minutes). Add the potato, pour over the stock or water, cover and bring to the boil and then cook for 10 minutes. Add the broccoli florets and cook for 3 minutes. Then add the peas and cook for a further 3 minutes. Purée in a mouli.

You could also make this purée using other green vegetables, like spinach or courgette.

Sweet potato with spinach and peas

Melt the butter in a saucepan and sauté the leeks for 3–4 minutes or until softened, then add the sweet potato. Pour over 200 ml (7 fl oz) water, bring to the boil, then cover and simmer for 7–8 minutes. Add the peas and spinach and cook for 3 minutes.

Purée the vegetables in a blender to make a smooth consistency, adding a little of the cooking liquid if necessary.

✏ 7 MINUTES

🍳 15 MINUTES

🍪 5 PORTIONS

❄ SUITABLE FOR FREEZING

25 g (1 oz) unsalted butter
50 g (2 oz) leeks, washed and finely sliced
375 g (13 oz) sweet potato, peeled and chopped
50 g (2 oz) frozen peas
75 g (3 oz) fresh baby spinach, washed and any tough stalks removed

Combining spinach with a sweet-tasting vegetable, like sweet potato, is a good way to introduce it to your baby. If you wish, you could use broccoli instead of spinach.

lentil and vegetable purée

✏️ 10 MINUTES
🖥️ 20 MINUTES
🍽️ 3 PORTIONS
❄️ SUITABLE FOR FREEZING

1 tablespoon olive oil
50 g (2 oz) leek, finely chopped
½ medium carrot (50 g/2 oz), finely chopped
½ garlic clove, crushed
50 g (2 oz) tinned green lentils, drained and rinsed
200 g (7 oz) tinned chopped tomatoes
100 ml (3½ fl oz) water
1 teaspoon tomato purée
1 small bay leaf
1 ready-to-eat dried apricot, chopped
1 tablespoon chopped basil
2 tablespoons natural yoghurt (full fat)

Heat the oil in a saucepan. Add the leek, carrot and garlic. Sauté for 5 minutes. Add the lentils, tomatoes, water, tomato purée, bay leaf and apricot. Bring to the boil. Cover and simmer for 8–10 minutes.

Whiz using a hand blender until smooth. Stir in the basil and yoghurt.

This is a speedy recipe, as it uses tinned lentils, which are already cooked.

Carrot purée with lentils and cheese

Heat the oil in a large saucepan and sauté the onion until softened. Rinse the lentils and drain and add to the onion. Add the carrots and pour over 400 ml (14 fl oz) boiling water. Bring back to the boil, then cover and simmer over a medium heat for 25 minutes.

Meanwhile, melt the butter in a small saucepan and sauté the tomatoes until mushy, then stir in the Cheddar cheese.

Drain the carrot and lentil mixture, reserving the cooking liquid. Transfer the mixture to a food processor together with 125 ml (4 fl oz) of the cooking liquid and the tomato and cheese mixture. Purée to a smooth consistency.

✎ 7 MINUTES

▦ 30 MINUTES

🕐 4 PORTIONS

❄ SUITABLE FOR FREEZING

½ tablespoon vegetable oil
1 small onion (50 g/
   2 oz), peeled and finely
   chopped
25 g (1 oz) red lentils
2 medium carrots (200 g/
   7 oz), peeled and sliced
15 g (½ oz) unsalted butter
2 tomatoes, skinned (see
   box, left), deseeded and
   roughly chopped
50 g (2 oz) Cheddar cheese,
   grated

To remove the skin from a tomato, cut a cross in the base using a sharp knife. Put in a bowl and cover with boiling water. Leave for 1 minute. Drain and rinse in cold water. The skin should peel off easily.

lovely lentils

⟋ 7 MINUTES

▦ 30 MINUTES

◔ 5 PORTIONS

✹ SUITABLE FOR FREEZING

1 tablespoon sunflower oil
1 small onion (50 g/2 oz),
    peeled and finely chopped
1 medium carrot (100 g/
    3½ oz), chopped
15 g (½ oz) celery, washed
    and chopped
50 g (2 oz) split red lentils,
    rinsed
1 medium sweet potato
    (225 g/8 oz), peeled and
    chopped
300 ml (½ pint) unsalted
    vegetable stock or water
30 g (1 oz) Cheddar cheese,
    grated

Heat the oil and sauté the onion, carrot and celery for about 5 minutes, or until softened. Add the lentils and sauté for 1 minute. Stir in the sweet potato and pour over the stock or water. Bring to the boil, turn down the heat and simmer, covered, for about 20 minutes, or until the lentils are soft.

Purée in a blender and stir in the grated cheese until melted.

Lentil purées are delicious and very popular with babies. Lentils are rich in protein and iron and are especially good to include in your baby's diet if you're bringing him up as a vegetarian.

Vegetables with cheese sauce

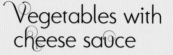

🖊 5 MINUTES

🗔 10 MINUTES

🕰 4 PORTIONS

❄ SUITABLE FOR FREEZING

75 g (3 oz) cauliflower, cut
  into florets
50 g (2 oz) broccoli, cut into
  florets
1 medium carrot (100 g/
  3½ oz), peeled and sliced
50 g (2 oz) frozen peas

Cheese sauce
15 g (½ oz) unsalted butter
15 g (½ oz) flour
200 ml (7 fl oz) milk
40 g (1½ oz) Cheddar cheese,
  grated

Put the cauliflower, broccoli and carrot into a
steamer set over a pan of boiling water and cook
for 4 minutes. Add the frozen peas and continue
to cook for 3 minutes.

Meanwhile, make the cheese sauce. Melt the
butter in a saucepan, stir in the flour to make a
smooth paste and cook for 1 minute. Gradually
stir in the milk, bring to the boil and cook for a
few minutes over a low heat until thickened and
smooth. Stir in the grated cheese until melted.

Pour the sauce over the vegetables and blend
to a purée or, for older babies, chop the
vegetables, then mix with the sauce. For young
babies, you can add a little more milk to thin the
purée, if necessary. Spoon a little into your baby's
bowl and serve lukewarm.

*Although your baby should have breast or formula
milk for the whole of the first year, you can use
cow's milk in cooking.*

Vegetable purée with tomato and cheese

Put the carrots into a steamer set over a pan of boiling water and steam for 14 minutes. Then add the cauliflower and steam for a further 6 minutes.

Meanwhile, melt the butter in a pan and sauté the tomatoes for about 2 minutes, until slightly mushy, then stir in the grated cheese until melted.

Blend the vegetables together with the cheese and tomato.

6 MINUTES

20 MINUTES

6 PORTIONS

NOT SUITABLE FOR FREEZING

2 medium carrots (200 g/ 7 oz), peeled and sliced
100 g (3½ oz) cauliflower, cut into small florets
a generous knob of unsalted butter
3 tomatoes, skinned, deseeded and roughly chopped
75 g (3 oz) Cheddar cheese, grated

Cauliflower contains glucosinolates, which are sulphurous compounds that help to protect against certain forms of cancer.

Carrot, sweet potato and broccoli

🔪 7 MINUTES

🍳 20 MINUTES

🕒 5 PORTIONS

❄️ SUITABLE FOR FREEZING

20 g (¾ oz) unsalted butter
75 g (3 oz) leek, peeled,
  washed and chopped
2 medium carrots (150 g/
  5 oz), peeled and chopped
150 g (5 oz) sweet potato,
  peeled and chopped
150 ml (¼ pint) milk
150 ml (¼ pint) water
50 g (2 oz) broccoli florets
25 g (1 oz) Parmesan cheese,
  grated

Melt the butter in a saucepan. Add the leek, carrot and sweet potato and fry for 3 minutes. Add the milk and water, bring to the boil, cover and simmer for 10 minutes. Add the broccoli and continue to simmer for 5 minutes, until the vegetables are soft.

Blend until smooth. Add the cheese and stir until melted.

Sweet vegetable trio

Put the vegetables into a steamer and cook for about 20 minutes, or until tender.

Alternatively, put the vegetables into a saucepan and cover with boiling water. Bring back to the boil, then reduce the heat, cover and simmer for about 20 minutes, or until tender.

Drain the vegetables, then blend using a hand blender. Add the milk and grated cheese and mix until smooth.

 10 MINUTES

20 MINUTES

3–4 PORTIONS

SUITABLE FOR FREEZING

150 g (5 oz) butternut squash, peeled, deseeded and chopped

1 parsnip (75 g/3 oz), peeled and chopped

2 medium carrots (150 g/ 5 oz), peeled and chopped

3 tablespoons milk

1 tablespoon Cheddar cheese, grated

Root vegetables have a natural sweetness that babies like and they are easy to digest.

Mediterranean medley

✎ 12 MINUTES

▦ 30 MINUTES

🍽 8 PORTIONS

❋ SUITABLE FOR FREEZING

1 tablespoon olive oil
1 medium onion (140 g/
   5 oz), peeled and chopped
1 small courgette
   (125 g/4½ oz), washed
   and chopped
½ red pepper (50 g/2 oz),
   washed, deseeded and
   chopped
75 g (3 oz) aubergine,
   washed and chopped
1 garlic clove, crushed
175 g (6 oz) butternut
   squash, peeled, deseeded
   and chopped
400 g (14 oz) tinned
   chopped tomatoes
100 ml (3½ fl oz) water
2 tablespoons chopped basil
40 g (1½ oz) Cheddar cheese,
   grated

Heat the oil in a saucepan. Add the onion and fry for 2 minutes. Add the courgette, pepper, aubergine and garlic and fry for 3 minutes. Add the squash, tomatoes and water. Bring to the boil, then cover and simmer for 20 minutes, until the vegetables are soft. Add the basil, then blend until smooth. For older babies, you can simply mash the vegetables with a fork. Add the Cheddar and stir until melted.

It is important not to add any salt to your baby's food. Garlic and herbs are a good means of adding flavour.

Fish

Fillet of plaice with carrots, cheese and tomatoes

Put the carrots in a steamer set over a pan of boiling water and cook for 20 minutes.

Meanwhile, place the fish in a microwave-proof dish, add the milk, dot with 15 g (½ oz) of the butter and cover, leaving an air vent. Microwave on high for 2–3 minutes. Alternatively, put the fish in a pan, cover with a little milk and poach for about 5 minutes, or until cooked.

Melt the remaining butter in a saucepan, add the tomatoes and sauté until mushy. Stir in the cheese until melted.

Blend the carrots with the tomato mixture. Drain the cooking liquid and flake the fish, making sure there are no bones. Mix with the carrots and tomatoes. For younger babies, you can blend the fish together with the carrots and tomato for a smoother texture.

🔪 7 MINUTES

⬛ 25 MINUTES

🍪 4 PORTIONS

❄ SUITABLE FOR FREEZING

3 medium carrots (250 g/9 oz), peeled and sliced
225 g (8 oz) plaice fillets, skinned
2 tablespoons milk
40 g (1½ oz) unsalted butter
2 ripe tomatoes, skinned, deseeded and chopped
40 g (1½ oz) Cheddar cheese, grated

Plaice is one of the best fish to start with, as it has a suitably soft texture for young babies.

Lemon sole purée

🔪 15 MINUTES

🍳 20 MINUTES

🎨 5 PORTIONS

❄ SUITABLE FOR FREEZING

15 g (½ oz) unsalted butter
75 g (3 oz) leek, washed,
  peeled and chopped
2 medium carrots (150 g/5 oz),
  peeled and chopped
150 g (5 oz) potato, peeled
  and chopped
150 ml (¼ pint) milk
150 ml (¼ pint) water
150 g (5 oz) lemon sole fillet,
  skinned and cut into
  pieces
30 g (1 oz) spinach, washed
  and chopped
1 tablespoon chopped dill
1 teaspoon lemon juice
25 g (1 oz) Parmesan cheese,
  grated

Melt the butter in a saucepan. Add the leek,
carrot and potato and fry for 3 minutes. Add the
milk and water, bring to the boil, then cover and
simmer for 10 minutes. Add the lemon sole,
spinach, dill and lemon juice and simmer for
another 5 minutes.

Blend until smooth, then stir in the cheese
until melted.

*Fish is such a great food for babies. Try to introduce
it as soon as first tastes have been accepted. Fresh
dill adds a lovely flavour to this recipe.*

Tasty fish with sweet potato and orange

✎ 5 MINUTES

▦ 15 MINUTES

◷ 4 PORTIONS

✹ SUITABLE FOR FREEZING

1 sweet potato (about
   450 g/1 lb), peeled and
   chopped
175 g (6 oz) plaice fillets,
   skinned
juice of 1 orange (about
   100 ml/3½ fl oz)
50 g (2 oz) Cheddar cheese,
   grated
a knob of unsalted butter

Place the sweet potato in a steamer over a pan
of boiling water and cook for 10 minutes, or until
tender. Alternatively, put the sweet potato in a
pan, just cover with water and bring to the boil.
Then lower the heat and cook until tender.

Meanwhile, place the fish in a suitable
microwave-proof dish, pour over the orange juice
and scatter over the grated cheese. Cover, leaving
an air vent, and microwave on high for 3 minutes
or until the fish flakes easily with a fork.
Alternatively, you could place the fish and the
orange juice in a saucepan and poach for a few
minutes, until cooked, then stir in the grated
cheese until melted.

Flake the fish with a fork, checking to make
sure there are no bones. Mash the sweet potato
with a knob of butter and combine with the fish.

For young babies, you can purée the fish
together with the sweet potato.

Spoon some of the purée into your baby's
bowl and serve lukewarm.

Salmon surprise

Put the carrots into a saucepan, cover with water, bring to the boil and cook over a medium heat for about 20 minutes, until tender. Alternatively, place the carrots in a steamer and cook for 20 minutes.

Meanwhile, place the salmon in a microwave-proof dish, pour over the orange juice and scatter over the cheese. Cover, leaving an air vent, and microwave on high for about 2 minutes or until the fish flakes easily with a fork. Alternatively, cover with foil and cook in an oven preheated to 180°C/350°F/Gas 4 for about 20 minutes.

Reserve the cooking liquid, then flake the fish with a fork, carefully removing any bones.

Drain the carrots, mix with the butter and milk, then purée in a blender together with the flaked fish and the reserved liquid. For older babies, mash the carrots together with the butter and the milk, then mix in the flaked fish.

✐ 10 MINUTES

🗏 25 MINUTES

🍽 3 PORTIONS

❄ SUITABLE FOR FREEZING

2 medium carrots (200 g/ 7 oz), peeled and sliced
125 g (4½ oz) salmon fillet, skinned
60 ml (2 fl oz) orange juice
40 g (1½ oz) Cheddar cheese, grated
15 g (½ oz) unsalted butter
2 tablespoons milk

Squash, salmon and spinach

Heat the oil in a saucepan. Add the onion and fry for 3 minutes. Add the squash and water. Simmer for 15 minutes, until the squash is soft. Add the salmon and spinach and stir for 3 minutes, until the salmon is cooked and the spinach is wilted. Add the cream cheese, Parmesan and dill.

Blend until smooth using an electric hand blender.

🔪 10 MINUTES

🍳 25 MINUTES

🍽 4 PORTIONS

❄ SUITABLE FOR FREEZING

2 tablespoons sunflower oil
½ small onion (30 g/1 oz), peeled and chopped
200 g (7 oz) butternut squash, peeled, deseeded and chopped
350 ml (12 fl oz) water
225 g (8 oz) salmon fillet, skinned and chopped
50 g (2 oz) baby spinach, washed
2 tablespoons cream cheese
1 tablespoon Parmesan cheese, grated
2 teaspoons chopped dill

Oily fish like salmon provide a good source of essential fatty acids, which are important for the development of the brain, nervous system and vision. A baby's brain grows very rapidly in the first year.

Poached salmon with sweet potato and peas

/ 5 MINUTES

⊞ 15–17 MINUTES

◔ 3 PORTIONS

✳ SUITABLE FOR FREEZING

150 ml (¼ pint) unsalted
  vegetable stock or water
125 g (4½ oz) sweet potato,
  peeled and chopped
100 g (3½ oz) salmon fillet,
  skinned and cut into 1 cm
  (³⁄₈ in) cubes
2 tablespoons frozen peas
40 g (1½ oz) mature
  Cheddar cheese, grated

Put the stock or water into a saucepan with
the sweet potato. Bring to the boil, cover, then
simmer over a medium heat for 7–8 minutes,
or until the sweet potato is just tender. Add the
salmon and peas, cover again and simmer for
3–4 minutes, until the fish flakes easily and the
vegetables are tender. Remove from the heat
and stir in the cheese.

Blend to a purée for young babies or mash
for older babies.

*It's hard to find a jar of baby purée that contains
oily fish such as salmon, yet the essential fatty
acids it contains are incredibly important. Fats like
these are a major component of the brain; for this
reason, 50 per cent of the calories in breast milk
are composed of fat.*

Baby's first fish pie

Put the potato and onion into a saucepan. Cover with the milk and fish stock. Bring to the boil, cover and simmer for 10 minutes. Add the peas and cod, and continue to cook for 5 minutes.

Blend to a purée, then add the lemon juice, cheese and dill.

🔪 10 MINUTES

🔲 20 MINUTES

🍳 4 PORTIONS

❄️ SUITABLE FOR FREEZING

200 g (7 oz) potatoes, peeled
   and cut into chunks
1 small onion (60 g/2 oz),
   peeled and finely chopped
100 ml (3½ fl oz) milk
100 ml (3½ fl oz) unsalted
   fish stock
50 g (2 oz) frozen peas
150 g (5 oz) cod, skinned
   and cut into small cubes
1 teaspoon lemon juice
3 tablespoons grated
   Parmesan cheese
1 teaspoon chopped dill

Haddock, carrot and pea

Melt the butter in a saucepan. Add the onion, carrot and celery and fry for 5 minutes. Add the potato, water and milk. Bring to the boil, then cover and simmer for 15 minutes. Add the peas and haddock and simmer for another 4–5 minutes. Blend until smooth, then stir in the cheese.

🥄 10 MINUTES
🍳 30 MINUTES
🕐 5 PORTIONS
❄️ SUITABLE FOR FREEZING

20 g (¾ oz) unsalted butter
½ large onion (100 g/3½ oz), peeled and chopped
1 medium carrot (100 g/ 3½ oz), peeled and chopped
75 g (3 oz) celery, washed and chopped
175 g (6 oz) potato, peeled and chopped
200 ml (7 fl oz) water
150 ml (¼ pint) milk
50 g (2 oz) frozen peas
175 g (6 oz) haddock, skinned and chopped
50 g (2 oz) mature Cheddar cheese, grated

Cod with orange and squash

🔪 15 MINUTES

🗓 25 MINUTES

🍴 5 PORTIONS

❄ SUITABLE FOR FREEZING

1 tablespoon sunflower oil
½ medium onion (75 g/3 oz),
  peeled and chopped
30 g (1 oz) red pepper,
  washed, deseeded and
  chopped
150 g (5 oz) butternut
  squash, peeled, deseeded
  and chopped
75 g (3 oz) sweet potato,
  peeled and chopped
250 g (9 oz) tinned chopped
  tomatoes
5 tablespoons orange juice
250 ml (8 fl oz) water
150 g (5 oz) cod fillet,
  skinned and chopped

Heat the oil in a saucepan. Add the onion, pepper, butternut squash and sweet potato. Fry for 5 minutes. Add the tomatoes, orange juice and water. Bring to the boil, cover and simmer for 10 minutes. Add the cod and simmer for another 5 minutes. Blend until smooth.

Save yourself the hard work of peeling and chopping butternut squash. You can buy it peeled and ready-chopped in the supermarket.

Chicken

Chicken with sweet potato and apple

Heat the butter in a saucepan, add the onion, and sauté for 2–3 minutes. Add the chicken and sauté for a few minutes, until it turns opaque. Tip in the sweet potato and apple, and pour over the stock. Bring to the boil, then cover and simmer for 12 minutes. Purée to the desired consistency.

🔪 10 MINUTES

🍲 25 MINUTES

🍪 8 PORTIONS

❄️ SUITABLE FOR FREEZING

15 g (½ oz) unsalted butter
½ small onion (40 g/1½ oz), peeled and chopped
110 g (4 oz) chicken breast fillet, chopped
300 g (11 oz) sweet potato, peeled and chopped
½ dessert apple, peeled and chopped
200 ml (7 fl oz) unsalted chicken stock

Chicken is an ideal 'growth' food, as it's packed with protein and vitamin B12, which isn't found in plants.

Cherub's chowder

⟋ 6 MINUTES

▦ 16–17 MINUTES

✦ 5 PORTIONS

✦ SUITABLE FOR FREEZING

1 tablespoon vegetable oil
1 medium onion (about
    140 g/5 oz), peeled and
    chopped
225 g (8 oz) potatoes, peeled
    and cut into chunks
175 ml (6 fl oz) unsalted
    vegetable or chicken stock
50 g (2 oz) fresh or frozen
    sweetcorn
60 ml (2 fl oz) milk
50 g (2 oz) cooked chicken,
    finely chopped

Heat the oil in a saucepan and sauté the onion until soft. Add the potatoes and pour over the stock. Bring to the boil, then cover and simmer for about 12 minutes. Add the sweetcorn and the milk and simmer for a further 2–3 minutes.

Purée the chowder in a mouli, together with the chicken, and heat through.

Alternatively, for older babies, purée the onion and potato mixture in a mouli, then stir in the sweetcorn and the chicken.

To give the consistency of a soup, add a little extra milk and stock.

When puréed, sweetcorn husks tend to be a bit lumpy and difficult to digest, so for young babies I prefer to put it through a mouli. For older babies, I purée the potato mixture and then stir in the sweetcorn.

Chicken with butternut squash and tarragon

Melt the butter in a saucepan. Add the onion and sauté for 5 minutes, until softened. Add the butternut squash and chicken, and fry for about 5 minutes or until the chicken is opaque. Sprinkle over the flour, then blend in the milk. Bring to the boil, stirring until slightly thickened. Add the lemon zest and juice, cover and simmer for 10 minutes, until the squash is soft and the chicken is cooked through. Purée using a hand blender, then stir in the cheese and tarragon.

10 MINUTES

25 MINUTES

2 PORTIONS

SUITABLE FOR FREEZING

a knob of unsalted butter
½ large onion (100 g/3½ oz), peeled and finely chopped
100 g (3½ oz) butternut squash, peeled, deseeded and chopped
100 g (3½ oz) chicken breast fillet, cut into small pieces
1 tablespoon plain flour
100 ml (3½ fl oz) milk
a pinch of lemon zest
1 teaspoon lemon juice
1 tablespoon finely grated Parmesan cheese
a pinch of finely chopped tarragon

Annabel's chicken delight

/ 10 MINUTES

▦ 20 MINUTES

🍳 5 PORTIONS

❄ SUITABLE FOR FREEZING

1 tablespoon sunflower oil
½ medium red onion (75 g/
    3 oz), peeled and chopped
½ red pepper (50 g/2 oz),
    washed, deseeded and
    chopped
75 g (3 oz) apple, peeled,
    cored and chopped
1 medium carrot (100 g/
    3½ oz), peeled and chopped
150 g (5 oz) minced chicken
    or turkey
2 garlic cloves, crushed
10 g (¼ oz) prunes, chopped
½ teaspoon ground
    cinnamon
400 g (14 oz) tinned
    chopped tomatoes
150 ml (¼ pint) water
1 teaspoon tomato purée

Heat the oil in a frying pan. Add the onion, red
pepper, apple and carrot, and fry for 2 minutes.
Add the chicken or turkey, garlic, prunes and
cinnamon, and stir until the mince is browned.
Add the tomatoes, water and tomato purée.
Bring to the boil, then cover and simmer for
15 minutes. Blend until smooth.

*Prunes are a good source of instant energy, fibre
and iron. They help with constipation, as they're
a natural laxative.*

Creamy chicken with sweet potato

🔪 5 MINUTES

🍳 10 MINUTES

🍴 2 PORTIONS

❄️ SUITABLE FOR FREEZING

150 g (5 oz) sweet potato,
  peeled and chopped
10 g (¼ oz) unsalted butter
1 tablespoon plain flour
150 ml (¼ pint) milk
15 g (½ oz) Cheddar cheese,
  grated
30 g (1 oz) cooked chicken,
  chopped

Steam the sweet potato for about 10 minutes, or until tender.

Meanwhile, melt the butter in a small saucepan, stir in the flour to make a roux, then gradually stir in the milk. Bring to the boil and then reduce the heat and cook for a couple of minutes. Remove from the heat and stir in the grated cheese, until melted.

Whiz the sweet potato together with the chopped chicken and cheese sauce.

This is a great way to use up any left-over cooked chicken.

Chicken with Mediterranean vegetables

Heat the oil in a saucepan. Add the onion, pepper, aubergine and courgette. Fry for 3 minutes. Add the chicken and garlic, and continue to fry for 1 minute. Add the tomatoes, water, tomato purée and oregano. Bring to the boil, cover and simmer for 15 minutes. Blend until smooth.

 10 MINUTES

🗒 20 MINUTES

🕐 5 PORTIONS

❄ SUITABLE FOR FREEZING

1 tablespoon sunflower oil
½ medium onion (75 g/3 oz), peeled and chopped
1 small red pepper (75 g/ 3 oz), washed, deseeded and chopped
50 g (2 oz) aubergine, washed and chopped
½ courgette (75 g/3 oz), washed and chopped
100 g (3½ oz) chicken breast fillet, chopped
2 garlic cloves, crushed
400 g (14 oz) tinned chopped tomatoes
100 ml (3½ fl oz) water
2 teaspoons tomato purée
¼ teaspoon dried oregano

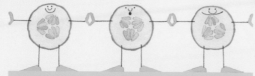

Mediterranean food is very healthy, so this is a good recipe to give your little one.

Chicken and sweetcorn

Heat the oil in a saucepan, add the onion and carrot, and fry for 3 minutes. Add the potato and sweet potato, chicken and sweetcorn, followed by the milk and water. Bring to the boil, cover and simmer for 15 minutes. Blend until smooth, then add the cheese, stirring until melted. Finally, stir in the lemon juice.

🍴 10 MINUTES
🍳 20 MINUTES
🕐 5 PORTIONS
❄️ SUITABLE FOR FREEZING

1 tablespoon sunflower oil
½ large onion (100 g/ 3½ oz), peeled and chopped
1 medium carrot (100 g/ 3½ oz), peeled and chopped
100 g (3½ oz) potato, peeled and cut into chunks
50 g (2 oz) sweet potato, peeled and chopped
100 g (3½ oz) chicken breast fillet, chopped
100 g (3½ oz) tinned or frozen sweetcorn
150 ml (¼ pint) milk
150 ml (¼ pint) water
25 g (1 oz) Parmesan cheese, grated
½ teaspoon lemon juice

Chicken with parsnip and sweet potato

🔪 12 MINUTES

🔲 25 MINUTES

🍽 4 PORTIONS

❄ SUITABLE FOR FREEZING

1 tablespoon sunflower oil
½ medium onion (75 g/
   3 oz), peeled and chopped
75 g (3 oz) celery, washed
   and chopped
1 medium carrot (100 g/
   3½ oz), peeled and chopped
100 g (3½ oz) sweet potato,
   peeled and chopped
1 medium parsnip (75 g/
   3 oz), peeled and chopped
150 g (5 oz) chicken breast
   fillet, chopped
200 ml (7 fl oz) unsalted
   chicken stock
100 ml (3½ fl oz) milk
25 g (1 oz) Parmesan cheese,
   grated

Heat the oil in a frying pan. Add the onion, celery, carrot, sweet potato and parsnip, and fry for 5 minutes. Add the chicken and fry for 1 minute. Add the stock and milk. Bring to the boil, then cover and simmer for 15 minutes. Stir in the Parmesan.

Beef

Beef with mushrooms, parsnip and sweet potato

Heat the oil in a saucepan. Add the onion and beef, and fry for 5 minutes. Add the mushrooms, carrot and parsnip, and fry until softened. Add the stock, thyme and tomato purée. Bring to the boil, then cover and simmer for 20 minutes.

Blend until smooth, then add the cheese and stir until melted.

🔪 10 MINUTES

⊞ 30 MINUTES

🍪 6 PORTIONS

❄ SUITABLE FOR FREEZING

1 tablespoon sunflower oil
½ large red onion (100 g/ 3½ oz), peeled and chopped
150 g (5 oz) minced beef
50 g (2 oz) chestnut mushrooms, washed and chopped
1 medium carrot (100 g/ 3½ oz), peeled and chopped
1 large parsnip (150 g/5 oz), peeled and chopped
400 ml (14 fl oz) unsalted beef stock
1 teaspoon chopped thyme
1 tablespoon tomato purée
25 g (1 oz) mature Cheddar cheese, grated

Red meat provides the best and most easily absorbed source of iron.

Braised beef with carrot, parsnip and sweet potato

🖌 12 MINUTES

🗂 1 HOUR 50 MINUTES

🍲 5 PORTIONS

❄ SUITABLE FOR FREEZING

1 tablespoon olive oil
½ medium onion (75 g/3 oz),
  peeled and chopped
1 garlic clove, crushed
150 g (5 oz) lean braising
  steak, cut into pieces
2 tablespoons flour
2 medium carrots (150 g/
  5 oz), peeled and sliced
1 medium parsnip (75 g/
  3 oz), peeled and sliced
250 g (9 oz) sweet potato,
  peeled and chopped
1 bay leaf
1 tablespoon chopped
  parsley
400 ml (14 fl oz) unsalted
  chicken stock

Heat the oil in a heavy-bottomed saucepan or small casserole dish. Sauté the onion and garlic for 3–4 minutes, until softened. Toss the pieces of steak in the flour and sauté until browned all over. Add the carrot, parsnip, sweet potato, bay leaf and parsley, and pour over the stock. Bring to the boil, cover and simmer over a low heat for about 1¾ hours or until the meat is tender.

Blend, using as much of the cooking liquid as required to achieve the desired consistency.

Babies can be put off red meat because they find it difficult to chew. Mixing it with root vegetables gives it a smooth texture and a flavour that makes the meat more appealing.

Beef with sweet pepper and tomato purée

Heat the oil in a saucepan. Add the red onion and pepper and sauté for 5 minutes, until nearly soft. Add the steak and ground coriander and fry for 2 minutes, until the meat is browned. Add the tomatoes and apple juice. Bring to the boil, then cover and simmer for 10 minutes.

Purée using a hand blender until completely smooth.

 5 MINUTES

▦ 20 MINUTES

🍽 2 PORTIONS

❄ SUITABLE FOR FREEZING

1 tablespoon olive oil
½ large red onion (100 g/ 3½ oz), peeled and finely chopped
½ red pepper (50 g/2 oz), washed, deseeded and finely chopped
50 g (2 oz) sirloin steak, cut into thin strips
a pinch of ground coriander
200 g (7 oz) tinned chopped tomatoes
2 teaspoons apple juice

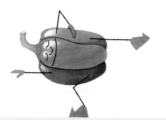

The iron a baby inherits from her mother runs out at six months, so it is important to introduce iron-rich foods as soon as possible once you start weaning.

Beef and carrot casserole

Heat a large saucepan and add the mince. Once the beef has browned, add the onion, carrots and celery. Fry for 3–4 minutes, until lightly golden. Sprinkle over the flour. Blend in the apple juice, stock and passata. Bring to the boil, and add the tomato purée and thyme. Cover and simmer over a low heat for 30 minutes, until tender. Add the Worcestershire sauce and Parmesan cheese, then blend to a purée (if desired).

8 MINUTES
40 MINUTES
5 PORTIONS
SUITABLE FOR FREEZING

200 g (7 oz) lean minced beef
1 large onion (185 g/6½ oz), peeled and finely chopped
2 small carrots (100 g/ 3½ oz), peeled and roughly chopped
1 stick celery, washed and finely chopped
1 tablespoon plain flour
50 ml (2 fl oz) apple juice
200 ml (7 fl oz) unsalted beef stock
100 ml (3½ fl oz) passata
1 teaspoon tomato purée
½ teaspoon dried thyme
a dash of Worcestershire sauce (optional)
10 g (¼ oz) Parmesan cheese, grated

Iron is important for your baby's brain development, especially between six months and two years.

Beef, carrot and sweet potato

✎ 7 MINUTES

▦ 30 MINUTES

✆ 6 PORTIONS

❇ SUITABLE FOR FREEZING

1 tablespoon sunflower oil
½ large red onion (100 g/
   3½ oz), peeled and chopped
1 medium carrot (100 g/
   3½ oz), peeled and chopped
150 g (5 oz) minced beef
2 garlic cloves, crushed
400 g (14 oz) tinned
   chopped tomatoes
10 g (¼ oz) prunes, chopped
200 ml (7 fl oz) water
1 bay leaf

Heat the oil in a saucepan. Add the onion and carrot and fry for 2 minutes. Add the beef, and brown with the vegetables. Add the garlic, tomatoes, prunes, water and bay leaf. Bring to the boil, cover and simmer for 20 minutes. Remove the bay leaf, then blend until smooth.

Adding dried fruit like prunes gives a hint of sweetness that babies like.

Baby beef casserole

Heat the oil in a pan. Add the onion and fry for 2 minutes. Add the mince, and brown. Add the garlic, sweet potato and carrot. Stir over the heat for 2 minutes. Add the tomatoes and water. Bring to the boil, then simmer for 30 minutes, until tender. Blend until smooth, then stir in the cheese.

🥄 7 MINUTES

🍳 35 MINUTES

🍽 4 PORTIONS

❄ SUITABLE FOR FREEZING

1 teaspoon olive oil
1 small onion (60 g/2 oz),
   peeled and chopped
50 g (2 oz) minced beef
¼ garlic clove, crushed
100 g (3½ oz) sweet potato,
   peeled and chopped
25 g (1 oz) carrot, peeled
   and chopped
400 g (14 oz) tinned
   chopped tomatoes
150 ml (¼ pint) water
25 g (1 oz) Cheddar cheese,
   grated

Pasta

Pasta shells with carrot and tomato

Steam the carrots for about 20 minutes, or until tender. Cook the baby pasta shells according to the packet instructions.

Meanwhile, heat the butter in a separate pan, then add the tomatoes and sauté until mushy. Remove from the heat and stir in the cheese until melted, then add the basil.

Using an electric hand blender, purée the carrots, together with 3 tablespoons of the liquid from the bottom of the steamer and the tomato and cheese mixture. Drain the pasta and stir into the carrot and tomato mixture.

🔪 8 MINUTES

🍳 20 MINUTES

🥧 4 PORTIONS

❄️ SUITABLE FOR FREEZING

2 small carrots (about 125 g/ 4½ oz), peeled and sliced
40 g (1½ oz) Annabel Karmel organic baby pasta shells
20 g (¾ oz) unsalted butter
3 medium tomatoes (about 225 g/8 oz), skinned, deseeded and quartered
40 g (1½ oz) Cheddar cheese, grated
2 fresh basil leaves, torn into pieces

Carrots are most nutritious when cooked with a little butter or oil, as the betacarotene they contain is absorbed by our bodies more readily. The same is true of tomatoes, which are rich in the powerful antioxidant lycopene.

Baby vegetable pasta

⏱ 10 MINUTES

📋 18 MINUTES

🍽 4 PORTIONS

❄ SUITABLE FOR FREEZING

50 g (2 oz) Annabel Karmel
  organic baby pasta shells
10 g (¼ oz) unsalted butter
1 small onion (50 g/2 oz),
  peeled and finely chopped
1 small carrot (30 g/1 oz),
  peeled and finely diced
30 g (1 oz) red pepper, finely
  diced
30 g (1 oz) frozen sweetcorn
30 g (1 oz) frozen peas
10 g (¼ oz) plain flour
250 ml (8 fl oz) unsalted
  vegetable stock
2 tablespoons chopped basil
1 teaspoon lemon juice
30 g (1 oz) Parmesan cheese,
  grated

Cook the pasta following the packet instructions, then drain.

Melt the butter in a saucepan. Add the onion, carrot and pepper, cover with a lid and sauté for 10 minutes, until nearly soft. Add the sweetcorn and peas and sauté for 2 minutes. Add the flour, then pour in the stock, stirring until thickened. Simmer for 3 minutes, then add the basil, lemon juice and Parmesan. Finally, stir in the pasta.

As your baby gets older, it's important to encourage him to chew. Dicing vegetables instead of puréeing them is a good way to do this.

Cheese sauce with butternut squash

First, infuse the milk. Put the milk, onion wedges, bay leaf, parsley stalks and peppercorns into a pan. Bring to the boil and simmer gently for 20–30 minutes, then strain through a sieve into a jug.

Cook the pasta according to the packet instructions, then drain.

Meanwhile, melt the butter in a clean saucepan. Add the carrot and squash, and sauté for 5 minutes. Add the flour, then the strained milk, stirring until thickened. Simmer for 10 minutes, until the ingredients are soft.

Blend the vegetables and sauce in a food processor, until smooth. For older babies, blend half the vegetables and chop the other half. Add the mustard and cheeses. Stir in the pasta.

Infusing the milk gives this sauce a nice flavour, but you can skip this step if you wish.

✎ 8 MINUTES

▦ 18 MINUTES (PLUS 20–30 MINUTES FOR INFUSING)

🍴 3 PORTIONS

❄ NOT SUITABLE FOR FREEZING

400 ml (14 fl oz) milk
½ small onion (40 g/ 1½ oz), peeled and cut into wedges
1 bay leaf
3 parsley stalks
3 peppercorns
60 g (2 oz) baby pasta shells
10 g (¼ oz) unsalted butter
1 medium carrot (75 g/3 oz), peeled and chopped
50 g (2 oz) squash, peeled, deseeded and chopped
10 g (¼ oz) plain flour
¾ teaspoon Dijon mustard
20 g (¾ oz) Parmesan cheese, grated
20 g (¾ oz) mature Cheddar cheese, grated

Tomato, sweet potato and cheese sauce with pasta shells

 10 MINUTES

🔲 40 MINUTES

🍪 6 PORTIONS

❄️ SUITABLE FOR FREEZING

1 tablespoon olive oil
1 medium onion (about
  140 g/5 oz), peeled and
  chopped
1 garlic clove, chopped
225 g (8 oz) sweet potato,
  peeled and chopped
2 small carrots (about 125 g/
  4½ oz), peeled and sliced
400 g (14 oz) tinned
  chopped tomatoes
200 ml (7 fl oz) unsalted
  vegetable stock or water
100 g (3½ oz) Annabel
  Karmel organic baby
  pasta shells
60 g (2 oz) Cheddar cheese,
  grated

Heat the oil in a saucepan and sauté the onion for about 4 minutes, until softened. Add the garlic and sauté for 1 more minute. Stir in the sweet potato and carrots, then stir in the tomatoes and stock or water. Bring to the boil, stirring, then cover and simmer for about 30 minutes, until the vegetables are tender.

Meanwhile, cook the pasta according to the packet instructions, then drain.

Once the sauce is cooked, allow to cool slightly, then blend to a purée and stir in the cheese until melted. Mix the drained pasta with the sauce.

Try blending this versatile sauce with fish or chicken instead of pasta.

Confetti pasta

Cook the pasta for 6 minutes, together with the carrot. Add the peas for the last 2–3 minutes of cooking time, then drain. Stir in the cream and Parmesan and serve.

🔪 5 MINUTES
🍳 9 MINUTES
🍽 2 PORTIONS
❄ NOT SUITABLE FOR FREEZING

50 g (2 oz) orzo or other small pasta shapes
1 small carrot (30 g/1 oz), peeled and diced
30 g (1 oz) frozen peas
1½ tablespoons single cream
3 tablespoons Parmesan cheese, grated

Peas belong to the super-veggie league. They're a great source of vitamins A and C, as well as folic acid and B vitamins.

Pasta shells with butternut squash and tomato sauce

✏️ 10 MINUTES

🍳 15 MINUTES

🍽️ 2 PORTIONS

❄️ SUITABLE FOR FREEZING

2 tablespoons Annabel
  Karmel organic baby
  pasta shells
150 g (5 oz) butternut
  squash, peeled, deseeded
  and chopped
15 g (½ oz) unsalted butter
3 medium tomatoes,
  skinned, deseeded and
  quartered
30 g (1 oz) Cheddar cheese,
  grated

Cook the pasta following the packet instructions. Steam the butternut squash for 10 minutes, or until tender.

Meanwhile, melt the butter in a small saucepan and sauté the tomatoes until mushy. Stir in the cheese until melted.

Blend the butternut squash with the tomato and cheese. Drain the pasta and stir into the sauce.

Adding small pasta shapes is a good way to gradually introduce more texture into your baby's food.

Lentil and tomato pasta

- 10 MINUTES
- 30 MINUTES
- 4 PORTIONS
- SUITABLE FOR FREEZING

1 tablespoon sunflower oil
½ medium onion (about
  75 g/3 oz), peeled and
  chopped
½ red pepper (50 g/2 oz),
  washed, deseeded and
  chopped
1 small carrot (50 g/2 oz),
  peeled and grated
¼ courgette (50 g/2 oz),
  washed, topped and tailed
  and chopped
1 garlic clove, crushed
3 tablespoons split red
  lentils, rinsed
200 g (7 oz) tinned chopped
  tomatoes
200 ml (7 fl oz) unsalted
  chicken stock
1 tablespoon sun-dried
  tomato paste
75 g (3 oz) Annabel Karmel
  organic baby pasta shells
25 g (1 oz) Parmesan cheese,
  grated

Heat the oil in a saucepan. Add the onion, pepper, carrot and courgette, and fry for 3 minutes. Add the garlic and fry for 30 seconds. Add the lentils, then the tomatoes, stock and sun-dried tomato paste. Bring to the boil, cover and simmer for 25 minutes.

Meanwhile, cook the pasta according to the packet instructions, then drain.

Blend the lentils and vegetables until smooth, using an electric hand blender. Stir in the Parmesan cheese and mix in the pasta.

Lentils are a good source of protein and fibre. They are also rich in potassium, zinc and folic acid.

Pasta with carrot and courgette

Cook the pasta following the packet instructions, then drain.

Meanwhile, heat the oil in a saucepan. Add the onion, carrot and courgette, and fry for 8 minutes, until soft. Add the garlic and fry for 30 seconds. Add the stock and pasta, and stir over the heat. Mix in the Parmesan, basil and crème fraîche.

/ 8 MINUTES

☐ 10 MINUTES

3 PORTIONS

SUITABLE FOR FREEZING

75 g (3 oz) baby pasta shapes
1 tablespoon sunflower oil
½ medium onion (about 75 g/3 oz), peeled and chopped
1 medium carrot (about 100 g/3½ oz), peeled and grated
1 small courgette (about 100 g/3½ oz), washed, peeled and grated
1 small garlic clove, crushed
200 ml (7 fl oz) unsalted chicken stock
25 g (1 oz) Parmesan cheese, grated
1 tablespoon chopped basil
2 tablespoons crème fraîche

Little stars with minced beef

Cook the pasta following the packet instructions, then drain.

Melt the butter in a saucepan, add the onion, carrot and celery, and sauté for 5 minutes. Add the mince, and brown for 5 minutes, breaking up the lumps with a fork as you stir. Add the redcurrant jelly and sauté for 1 minute. Add the flour, then the stock, tomato purée, Worcestershire sauce and thyme. Simmer for 10 minutes, uncovered. Stir in the pasta.

/ 10 MINUTES

▭ 25 MINUTES

③ 3 PORTIONS

✱ SUITABLE FOR FREEZING

60 g (2 oz) pasta stars
10 g (¼ oz) unsalted butter
½ small onion (30 g/1 oz),
   peeled and finely chopped
1 small carrot (50 g/2 oz),
   peeled and finely chopped
30 g (1 oz) celery, washed
   and finely chopped
75 g (3 oz) minced beef
½ teaspoon redcurrant jelly
10 g (¼ oz) plain flour
250 ml (8 fl oz) unsalted
   beef stock
1 teaspoon tomato purée
1 teaspoon Worcestershire
   sauce
½ teaspoon chopped thyme

10 MINUTES

45–50 MINUTES

6 PORTIONS

SUITABLE FOR FREEZING

100 g (3½ oz) baby pasta shapes
1 teaspoon sunflower oil
1 small onion (60 g/2 oz), peeled and chopped
1 medium carrot (about 100 g/3½ oz), peeled and grated
½ red pepper (about 50 g/2 oz), washed, deseeded and chopped
1 garlic clove, crushed
175 g (6 oz) minced beef
400 g (14 oz) tinned chopped tomatoes
100 ml (3½ fl oz) unsalted beef stock
100 ml (3½ fl oz) apple juice
1 teaspoon chopped thyme
1 bay leaf
1 tablespoon sun-dried tomato paste
25 g (1 oz) Parmesan cheese, grated

Baby Bolognese

Cook the pasta following the packet instructions, then drain.

Meanwhile, heat the oil in a saucepan. Add the onion, carrot and pepper and fry for 3 minutes. Add the garlic, then the minced beef. Brown over the heat. Add all the remaining ingredients except for the Parmesan. Bring to the boil, cover and simmer for 35–40 minutes.

Remove the bay leaf, then transfer one third of the mixture and blend using a hand blender. Return to the pan with the remainder of the sauce, and mix with the pasta and cheese.

Fruit

My favourite porridge

Put the milk, porridge oats and apricots into a small saucepan. Bring to the boil, then simmer, stirring occasionally, for 3 minutes. Purée with the chopped pear using a hand-held electric blender.

🔪 3 MINUTES

⬜ 5 MINUTES

🍽 4 PORTIONS

❄ SUITABLE FOR FREEZING

150 ml (¼ pint) milk
15 g (½ oz) porridge oats
6 ready-to-eat dried
  apricots, chopped
1 large ripe pear, peeled,
  cored and chopped

Banana and fig porridge

/ 2 MINUTES

▢ 7 MINUTES

🍽 1 PORTION

❄ NOT SUITABLE FOR FREEZING

2 tablespoons porridge oats
2 soft, ready-to-eat dried
    figs, chopped
175 ml (6 fl oz) water
1 small banana

Put the oats into a small saucepan with the figs.
Pour over the water and bring to the boil. Reduce
the heat, cover and simmer for 5 minutes. Purée
and press through a sieve. Mash the banana and
mix with the porridge.

Spoon some of the porridge
into your baby's bowl and
allow to cool before serving.

Apple, pear and prune with oats

Put the oats, apple juice and water in a saucepan, bring to the boil and simmer for 2 minutes. Add the apple, prunes and pear, cover and simmer for 3 minutes, stirring occasionally. Purée to the desired consistency.

🖊 5 MINUTES

🖼 6 MINUTES

🍽 2 PORTIONS

❄ SUITABLE FOR FREEZING

2 tablespoons porridge oats
4 tablespoons pure, unsweetened apple juice
2 tablespoons water
1 small dessert apple, peeled, cored and chopped
2 prunes, stoned and chopped
1 small ripe pear, peeled, cored and chopped

You could make this recipe using soft, ready-to-eat dried figs instead of prunes.

Porridge, banana, peach and apricot

✎ 4 MINUTES

▭ 7 MINUTES

🍴 3 PORTIONS

❄ NOT SUITABLE FOR FREEZING

Put the milk, porridge and apricots into a small saucepan. Bring to the boil and simmer for a few minutes, stirring until the porridge is cooked. Add the peach and banana, and simmer for 2 minutes. Blend until smooth.

150 ml (¼ pint) milk
20 g (¾ oz) porridge oats
25 g (1 oz) dried apricots, chopped
1 ripe peach (150 g/5 oz), skinned (*see box, below left*), stoned and chopped
2 small bananas, peeled and sliced

Nectarine and apple

✎ 4 MINUTES

▭ 9–11 MINUTES

🍴 2 PORTIONS

❄ SUITABLE FOR FREEZING

Melt the butter in a small saucepan. Add the fruits and apple juice. Simmer for 8–10 minutes, until soft, then blend until smooth.

To remove the skin from any soft fruit, such as a peach, cut a cross in the base using a sharp knife. Put in a bowl and cover with boiling water. Leave for 1 minute. Drain and rinse in cold water. The skin should peel off easily.

a knob of unsalted butter
1 nectarine (150 g/5 oz), skinned (*see box, left*), stoned and chopped
1 dessert apple (100 g/3½ oz), peeled, cored and chopped
3 tablespoons apple juice

Left: Nectarine and apple

5 MINUTES

🔲 7 MINUTES

🍽 2 PORTIONS

❄ SUITABLE FOR FREEZING

a knob of unsalted butter
3 ripe plums, skinned,
  stoned and chopped
1 peach, skinned, stoned
  and chopped
20 g (¾ oz) prunes, stoned
  and chopped
1 tablespoon apple juice

Plum, peach and prune

Melt the butter in a small saucepan. Add the plums, peach, prunes and apple juice. Stir over the heat, then simmer for 5 minutes, until soft. Blend until smooth.

Apple, pear and plum with cinnamon

 6 MINUTES

🔲 4–5 MINUTES

🍽 2 PORTIONS

❄ SUITABLE FOR FREEZING

1 dessert apple, peeled,
  cored and chopped
1 large ripe pear, peeled,
  cored and chopped
2 ripe plums, skinned,
  stoned and chopped
a good pinch of cinnamon
2 tablespoons ricotta or
  Greek yoghurt (optional)

Put the fruit in a small saucepan, together with a tablespoon of water and the cinnamon. Cover and cook over a low heat for 4–5 minutes. Purée in a blender. If using, stir in the ricotta or Greek yoghurt, and then spoon some of the purée into your baby's bowl and serve lukewarm.

You could use 4 ready-to-eat stoned prunes rather than plums – a particularly good idea if your baby is constipated.

Right: Plum, peach and prune

Strawberry and banana

Measure all of the ingredients into a jug. Blend until smooth using a hand blender.

✎ 4 MINUTES

🍽 2 PORTIONS

❄ SUITABLE FOR FREEZING

150 g (5 oz) strawberries, hulled and halved
2 small bananas, peeled and sliced
2 tablespoons apple juice

Strawberry, peach and pear crumble

Put the fruit into a small, heavy-based saucepan, then cover and cook for about 3 minutes.

Crush the rusk by placing it in a plastic bag and banging it with a rolling pin.

Blend the fruit together with the rusk.

✎ 8 MINUTES

▦ 3 MINUTES

🍽 2 PORTIONS

❄ SUITABLE FOR FREEZING

75 g (3 oz) strawberries, hulled and quartered
1 large, juicy ripe peach, skinned, stoned and chopped
1 large ripe pear, peeled, cored and chopped
1 baby rusk

> *Some fruit purées are very runny, but you can thicken them by stirring in some baby rice, mashed banana or crumbled rusk, as here.*

Meal planner

	Day 1	Day 2	Day 3
Breakfast	**My favourite porridge** Milk	Baby cereal with milk **Nectarine and apple** Milk	**Apple, pear and prune with oats** Milk
Mid-morning	Milk	Milk	Milk
Lunch	**Lemon sole purée**	**Annabel's chicken delight**	**Beef, carrot and sweet potato**
Mid-afternoon	Milk	Milk	Milk
Dinner	**Carrot, sweet potato and broccoli**	**Pasta shells with butternut squash and tomato sauce**	**Lovely lentils**
Bedtime	Milk	Milk	Milk

This meal planner is intended to be used as a guide.
It's fine to give the same meal more than once in the
same week. Give water or diluted fruit juice with lunch
and dinner.

Day 4	Day 5	Day 6	Day 7
Porridge, banana, peach and apricot Milk	Well-cooked scrambled egg Milk	Strawberry, peach and pear crumble Milk	Weetabix Plum, peach and prune Milk
Milk	Milk	Milk	Milk
Cod with orange and squash	Chicken with sweet potato and apple	Braised beef with carrot, parsnip and sweet potato	Chicken and sweetcorn
Milk	Milk	Milk	Milk
Pasta shells with carrot and tomato	Haddock, carrot and pea	Sweet potato with spinach and peas	Baby Bolognese
Milk	Milk	Milk	Milk

Between six and nine months, your baby will probably start to self-feed finger foods. Give toast, chunks of soft fruit and steamed or raw vegetables to supplement the meals suggested above.

Index

About Annabel Karmel

Mother of three, Annabel Karmel MBE is the UK's number one parenting author and expert on devising delicious, nutritious meals for babies, toddlers and children.

Since launching with *The Complete Baby and Toddler Meal Planner* more than two decades ago, Annabel has written 37 books, which have sold over 4 million copies worldwide, covering every stage of a child's development.

With the sole aim of helping parents give their children the very best start in life, Annabel's tried-and-tested recipes have also grown into a successful supermarket food range. From delicious Organic Baby Purées to her best-selling healthy chilled meals, these offer the goodness of a home-cooked meal for those busy days.

Annabel was awarded an MBE in 2006, in the Queen's Birthday Honours, for her outstanding work in child nutrition. She also has menus in some of the largest leisure resorts in Britain and a successful app, *Annabel's Essential Guide to Feeding Your Baby and Toddler*.

For more information and recipes, visit **www.annabelkarmel.com**.

Acknowledgements

Louise Ward and Phil Carroll (Sainsbury's Books), Fiona MacIntyre, Martin Higgins and Cat Dowlett (Ebury), Dave King (photography), Tamsin Weston (props), Kate Bliman and Maud Eden (food stylists), Lucinda McCord (recipe testing), Nick Eddison and Katie Golsby (Eddison Sadd), and Sarah Smith (PR).

annabel karmel

Other titles in the series are:

ANNABEL KARMEL'S FAVOURITES
First foods
Recipes and advice to help you wean your baby
Suitable from four months

ANNABEL KARMEL'S FAVOURITES
Growing independence
Healthy home-made recipes to encourage self-feeding
Suitable from nine to twelve months

ANNABEL KARMEL'S FAVOURITES
Toddler meals
Nutritious recipes for your child to enjoy with the family
Suitable from one year

ANNABEL KARMEL'S FAVOURITES
Lunchboxes
Quick, easy and healthy ideas to make lunchtime fun
50 healthy recipes

ANNABEL KARMEL'S FAVOURITES
Tasty food for fussy kids
Great recipes to tempt your picky eater
50 healthy recipes

ANNABEL KARMEL'S FAVOURITES
Family meals
Quick and easy recipes to keep meal times fresh
50 healthy recipes

ANNABEL KARMEL'S FAVOURITES
Vegetarian meals
Delicious, nutritious recipes for veggie kids
50 healthy recipes

ANNABEL KARMEL'S FAVOURITES
Party food
Quick, quirky and fun ideas for your child's celebration
50 healthy recipes

ANNABEL KARMEL'S FAVOURITES
Kids in the Kitchen
Creative recipe ideas to make and bake together
50 healthy recipes